Grade 1

Scott Foresman

Decodable
Readers 49-60
Unit 5

PEARSON
Scott
Foresman

Editorial Offices: Glenview, Illinois • Parsippany, New Jersey
New York, New York
Sales Offices: Needham, Massachusetts • Duluth, Georgia • Glenview,
Illinois • Coppell, Texas • Sacramento, California • Mesa, Arizona

ISBN: 0-328-14504-1

6 7 8 9 10 V054 14 13 12 11 10 09 08 07

Contents

A Day at the Fun Park

Written by Tessa Johnson
Illustrated by Phil Richard

Phonics Skill

Vowel Diphthong ow/ou/

now	crowd	clown(s)	how
down	frown	brown	

"The sun is up!"
Dan yelled.
He jumped up
and got dressed.

2

"Mom! Dad!
Let's eat fast," Dan begged.
"We must go now!
A big crowd will be there."

Dan and his mom and dad
drove to the fun park.
"It's a clown," Dan said.
"Let's go."

4

How does the clown walk on that rope?
He has big feet.
"Clowns walk slowly," said Mom.
Then the clown jumped down.

Dan liked that clown.
He was very funny.
He made Dan laugh.
Dan had no frown.

Dan and his mom and dad
went out to their brown car.
It was time to go home.

They came home at last.
Dan had lots of fun.
"That fun park is the best!" he said.

Decodable Reader 50

The Great Shirt

Written by Eric Weiss
Illustrated by Tony Ross

Phonics Skill

Consonant + le

little simple bundle sample dimple

Jen will start school soon.
She needs new stuff.
She was happy.
So was her mom.

10

Jen's mom planned on
getting a shirt for Jen.
They went shopping
at the mall.

Jen tried on a brown shirt.
It was too little.
Jen tried on a red shirt.
It was too big.

12

Jen tried on a simple blue shirt.
It had a big rip.
She did not see
a shirt she liked.

13

Her mom asked the clerk
if he had a cute shirt for Jen.
He got a bundle of
shirts to sample.

14

A green shirt in the bundle
fit Jen nicely.
It was not too little or too big.

Jen's smile was so big
that her dimple showed.
She gave her mom a big hug.

16

Rob Can Ride!

Written by Laura Susin
Illustrated by Victor Goosemen

Phonics Skill
Diphthong ou/ou/

outside   shouted   found   ouch   mouth

Rob likes to ride his bike.
Rob cannot ride inside.
He will ride outside.

Dad can help Rob ride.
"Hang on," shouted Dad.
Dad can run by
Rob as he rides.

Dad stopped running.
Rob is afraid.
Can he ride by himself?
He has never tried.

Rob found he can ride
by himself.
Rob rides quickly down the sidewalk.

Ouch! Rob fell.
He had to cry a little.
"Smile!" said Dad.
"Be happy you can ride."

Rob's mouth turned
from a frown to a smile.
Rob got up and dusted himself off.
He will still ride his bike.

Rob will ride his bike
back up the sidewalk by himself!
He will try his best to ride safely,
and he will smile all the way.

24

Pam's Happy Feet

Written by Jamey Ryndak
Illustrated by Peter Kronce

Phonics Skill
Syllables VCV

lemon   open(s)   begins   limit

Pam will start
dance class.
Pam is afraid.
Will she fit in?

"What a sour face!" said Mom.
"Did you eat a lemon?
Smile! It will be fun."
Mom pats Pam's cheek.

Pam will try to dance.
Pam will step with her feet.
She will swing her
arms behind her.

28

Pam will bring her hands high
and open them.
All of the girls do the same.

Class ends so fast!
Pam opens her mouth.
She begins to smile.
She is happy.

Pam can dance now!
She will not frown and look sour.
Her feet are happy at class!
Pam loves to dance.

31

Pam can dance all day.
She bends, turns, spins, and glides.
At home there is no limit.

The Animal Park

Written by Peter Brooks
Illustrated by Dan Vick

Phonics Skill

Vowels oo as in book

look(ed)	book	brook	wood
good	stood	took	

In class we looked at a book
about the park.
There is so much
to see at a park!

We will go to this park.
Our class hopes
we will see everything.
We hope there is time to play!

35

Look in this grass.
Snakes glide back and forth.
Black eyes shine bright.

Birds sit up high.
Look at that long branch.
Birds fly high in the sky.

Look at that gray fox by that brook!
He is much bigger
than he looked in that book.

Look at the three snails!
We like them best.
They go so slow along the wood!

It was a good day
at the park.
We stood and took a picture so that
we can remember our fun day.

40

The Family Camping Trip

Written by Drew Copperfield
Illustrated by Erica Thoem

Phonics Skill

*Inflected Endings -s, -es, -ed, -ing
(Including Spelling Change: drop e)*

camps	named	liked	looked
smiled	showed	walking	hiking
raced	fishing	camping	

My family camps out.
We go to the woods.
We cook outside
and sleep in tents.

Last time we went,
we left at sunrise.
Dad, Mom, Ben, Jake, and I
got in our car.
I slept all the way.

The woods are in a park.
That park is named
Grand Lake State Park.
I liked it very much.

The leaves on the trees
were nice colors.
The lake looked fine
in the sunshine.
We all smiled.

45

A map in our book
showed walking paths.
We went hiking.
Dad set up our tents
and made good lunches.

46

We raced to the big lake.
Mom said we could
go fishing the next day.
We got a huge fish!

Our camping trip
was fun.
We cannot wait
for our next camping trip.

48

Matt Helps Out!

Written by Frank Garcia
Illustrated by Fred McKann

Phonics Skill

Diphthong /oi/: oi, oy

| boy | voice | points | noise | soil | oinks |

Matt is a nice boy.
He likes to have fun.
He likes to help too.
How does he help?

Matt is riding his bike
down the road.
It is a nice day.
The sun is out.

There is a funny sound.
Matt stops his bike.
What can it be?
Is it a voice?

Matt points his bike
toward that funny sound.
He rides to the noise.

It is a big pig!
It is stuck
in soft, wet soil.

The pig oinks and squeals.
Matt wants to help.
Matt pulls that big pig.
Matt pushes that big pig.

At last the pig gets out!
Matt falls on the wet soil.
He gets mud on his legs.
But he is happy because he helped.

What Do You Want to Be?

Written by Grace Hammond
Illustrated by Minerva Tamondong

Phonics Skill

Suffixes -er, -or

| teacher | actor | sailor | singer | doctor |

What will you be
when you grow up?
Kids can become anything
if they try hard.

Pete will be a teacher.
He will teach reading and writing.
Pete likes school.
He is smart.

Jen will be an actor.
She will act on stage.
Jen is funny.
She is not shy.

Tom will be a sailor.
He will work on a ship.
Tom likes sailing.
He likes feeling the wind on his face.

Dan will be a singer.
He will sing songs.
Dan has a nice voice.
He likes being on stage.

62

Kim will be a doctor.
She will help people.
She will work hard.
She likes science.

What is your dream?
You can be a teacher, an actor,
a sailor—or anything!

Sam and Max

Written by Marta Janns
Illustrated by Dan Vick

Phonics Skill

Vowel /ô/: aw

| lawn | paws | saw | draws | yawns |

Sam likes to walk his pet Max.
It is against the rules
to walk on the lawn.
Sam and Max walk
on the sidewalk instead.

66

Max needs a bath every week.
Sam keeps Max's fur clean.
He cleans Max's paws.

Sam saw Max
run away one day.
Sam tried to call him.

But Max did not
stay away for long.
He came back.
Max ran on the lawn.
He licked Sam's face.

Max is Sam's best friend.
He goes anywhere Sam goes.
Max can do fun things.
He can shake Sam's hand!

70

Sam draws pictures of Max.
Max has big ears and big paws.
Max looks happy
in Sam's pictures.

When Sam yawns,
Max knows it is bedtime.
Max curls up at the end
of Sam's bed.

Lee's Snowy Day

Written by Jackie Tyndall
Illustrated by Josh Newport

Phonics Skill

Short e: ea

| head | ready | breath | heavy | dead | bread |

Lee saw fluffy snowflakes fall.
She liked the snow.
She rushed to the door.

"I will put on my coat," she said.
"I will put this hat on my head.
I will pull on my boots.
Then I will be ready to play."

Lee went outside.
She could see her breath.
Lee looked at the snow.
It was bright in the sunlight.

76

Lee hopped across her yard.
She left footprints in the snow
on that lawn.

Lee came to her hiding place.
It was under a bush.
She crawled on her knees
to get inside.

The heavy snow on top
made it dark inside.
Lee pushed away dead leaves
and sat down.

Lee sat snugly in her cave.
But she smelled the sweet bread
that Mom was baking.
"Time for a snack," Lee said.

Bess Makes a Mess

Written by Amy Park
Illustrated by Robert Knuel

Phonics Skill

Prefixes un-, re-

unhelpful	unclean	unmade	untie
refill	unlocked	unkind	unlike

Bess can be very unhelpful.
We stay in the same room.
She leaves our room unclean.
What can I do?

82

Bess left her bed unmade.
It does not look nice.
I make her bed instead.
Oh, Bess!

Bess tied the laces
on my skates too tightly.
Now I cannot untie them.
Oh, Bess!

Bess did not refill
the blue ice tray.
Now there is no ice for drinks.
Oh, Bess!

Bess unlocked our bird's cage.
Now our bird is free.
What if he gets lost?
Oh, Bess!

Bess is not unkind.
She is very sweet.
But I like things clean,
and she is unlike me.

How can I help Bess?
I do not want Bess to be messy.
What will I do?

Old Jo

Written by Trevor Stanton
Illustrated by Kyle West

Phonics Skill

Long Vowel Patterns -ost, -old, -ind, -ild

post	old	most	gold	hold
unwinds	mild	wild	told	cold

At the end of this road,
at the top of a post,
is the home of Old Jo
and the things he loves most.

His nest made of straw
is the color of gold,
and he fills it with
all the food it can hold.

Old Jo grabs a twig
and unwinds a string,
and he ties them together
to make a nice swing.

He sings and caws
with his voice that is mild.
Then he flies in the sky
on a ride that is wild.

Old Jo has a coat
that is black, I am told.
He crows all day long—
on warm days or cold.

94

He does not undress
when he's ready for bed.
He just fluffs up his coat
and tucks down his head.

95

When you think of Old Jo—
his nest, swing, and all—
Think of the fun things
that you can recall.